Faith.
Fear.
Resilience.

How to Reclaim Your
Educational Life.

Published by ZL Publishing House
Book Cover Design by Sylinthia Roque

A CIP catalog record for this book is available from the Library of Congress.

Aisha Y. Taylor
    Faith. Fear. Resilience./ by Aisha Y. Taylor

To contact the author, please visit: www.AishaTaylor.org

ISBN-13: 978-1-7339974-3-0 (paperback)
ISBN-13: 978-1-7339974-4-7 (ebook)

Made in the USA
10 9 8 7 6 5 4 3 2 1

Faith.
Fear.
Resilience.

How to Reclaim Your Educational Life.

Aisha Y. Taylor

PUBLISHING
HOUSE

CONTENTS

ACKNOWLEDGMENTS

THANK YOU TO my Lord and Savior Jesus Christ who rerouted my path to fulfill the vision that was given to me to serve my purpose.

To my family and friends, thank you for always being my support system and encouraging me as I have attempted to conquer my life goals and dreams.

Thank you to my husband for enduring this journey, which was suddenly placed in our lives. The road has not always been a straight path, but oftentimes came with many turns and curves. You have held my hand, loved me through the process, and always assured me that we were going to be alright. I love you dearly for that!

To my son, father, mother, sister, brother, Godsister, and Godmother for always believing in me and making me feel like I can conquer anything I come across in life. I am forever grateful for your prayers and unconditional love. It has boosted my confidence and taught me to be a fearless woman.

ABOUT ME

MY NAME IS Aisha Y. Taylor. I am first a firm believer in Jesus Christ. I am a wife, mother, educator, and confidence coach who believes your gifts lead you to discover your purpose. I strive to be a God-fearing woman who seeks to serve and inspire any and everyone who comes within my visible and spiritual path. I am convinced that believers of Christ are not on this earth by chance but for a special mission, which is created just for you by Him.

I have inspired and motivated many people with my gift, which is to seek what God has purposed in their heart. It has led me to experience the good and the ugly in the field of education. My faith is what has brought me through the fire and why I continue to love what I do. In a career field ever so changing and becoming more unsafe despite the socioeconomic area, you have to make sure you are in it for the right reasons. You must remember your attitude and confidence in what you are doing day in and day out is affecting someone's life daily.

I enjoy serving and building confidence in teachers and students so they may both experience success. I take pride in my work and know the work I have done is not to please *man* but to fulfill my purpose. I am grateful for life's journey, both good and bad, because it has increased my *faith* and my relationship with Jesus Christ.

I have learned that every time I choose to face my fear and trust God, something amazing happens! He shows me that his word his true and keeps his promises to give me the desires of my heart as long as I seek him first. So, I have found staying in the comfort of the known, rather than going into the unknown, holds people back from doing things that, in the end, could benefit them. That is what separates us from being kind and becoming great! As a result, I decided to "take the leap" to see just what God has in store for me.

Therefore, like any passion you have, you may get discouraged at times and wonder if you're really in the right place. In the education field, we sometimes see things that are not in the best interest of students, very political, and just downright wrong! We must remember that we were called to be in that place, at that time, and to work with those students and staff members for a called reason. Even when you think you are not making a difference, you are. The same goes for even when you don't believe you're leading, you are!

As teachers, we have all experienced a time where we taught a lesson, we thought the students were not listening, and that our work was in vain. Only to find out weeks later or at the end of the year, a student confirms and shares with you how grateful they are for your efforts.

You are truly making a difference! We live for those rare moments. They give us strength, energy, and the courage to get back into the classroom with perhaps a class full of ungrateful students and fight through another day! Those moments make our hearts sing!

In this book, I will be walking you through my most fearful moment in the field of education. I consider this to be the worst point in my entire career. In this point of enlightenment, God tested my faith. It was my passion for working with students that inspired me to push through despite any circumstances.

It took the attributes of *Faith, Fear, and Resilience* to overcome this challenging time in my life. I share my story to encourage readers within the field of education and outside the profession to stay confident in your abilities and to bounce back and stay faithful to where God has called you to be in your life. I truly believe that God placed me in this career field for a reason. He has allowed me to endure the heartache and joys of working in a high "at-risk," stressful, fast-paced campus to teach me so many lessons. One of the challenges of working with "at-risk" students is they require ongoing intervention to succeed academically. At-risk students are students already labeled to fail one or more grades, experience low attendance, and will struggle to graduate. What can I say? I love what I do! I appreciate every relationship, lesson learned, and experience that I have encountered.

In the last few years, I have been an Instructional Leader, as well as an Assistant Principal. In this position, I have witnessed educational leaders making decisions under a political bureaucracy that does not serve the best interest of the students. My faith was tested, my confidence diminished, and there were times I thought about quitting, but something just would not allow me to do so. It was my commitment to educating the future generation and being a role model for successful students.

PART I

Telling My Educational Story

CHAPTER 1

My Worst Day in Education

ON THURSDAY, MAY 18, 2017, I was standing in the hallways of a High School talking to the principal and a new teacher candidate about working on the campus. In what appeared to be a normal school day, ended with three students walking out in handcuffs. I would also witness Houston Police officers barging in on the school campus, weapons drawn, and search dogs looking for two students suspected in a robbery. I had no clue what was happening, so I immediately turned to the candidate and told her, "Go back to my office, my secretary will take care of you until I am able to get back and meet with you." My heart was racing while I watched the police chase a student through the hallway as he dropped stolen money on the floor. The campus immediately went on lockdown.

A school lockdown consists of all students being in a confined area (typically the classroom) with no one out in the hallway. Thank God, it was only a small number of students left in the hallway at that time because they began yelling in excitement as they ran to pick up the money the alleged offender dropped in an effort to get rid of it. Even though my mind understood what I saw and knew what lockdown meant, it seems that my body for thirty seconds was in disbelief of what I was watching and what was happening. My heart was pounding. I was afraid for not only myself but for the students as I watched police officers on our campus pointing their weapons, running, and looking for the alleged student criminals.

The high school is a large campus with a total population of 2,800 students. It was estimated that 200 of those students were in the cafeteria eating lunch. Lunch was suddenly interrupted as we quickly had to herd students into the auditorium. Trying hard not to show signs of panic nor fear, our goal was to refrain from exposing students to the reality that was occurring on campus.

The students were in the auditorium flustered and questioning why was lunch being interrupted. I began to see faces of fear, worry, and confusion as they saw several police officers go up and down the aisles actively looking for two suspects. I was asked by the police to get on the microphone and make an announcement to the students to remove all hoodies, sit up straight, and please cooperate. As law enforcement proceeded to go up and down the aisles looking for their suspect, I was hoping this was all a mistake and would be over as quickly as it happened.

After several minutes of searching, a young man I had a close relationship with, as his principal, was chosen out of a crowd of hundreds of students to go with the police officers. The crowd booed and sighed in disbelief as he was escorted out in handcuffs. My heart sank as I tried to hold it together, still standing on the stage in front of hundreds of students.

I will never forget the look on the young man's mother's face when she was escorted into the school. She was an active, hardworking, parent of the community, and was well known in leadership. This mother tried to use all of her spare time to prevent this from happening to her son, and the unthinkable still occurred as she saw her son in handcuffs seated on the ground outside the school gym.

The incident caused local breaking news all over the city of Houston. The public now looked upon the campus in horror hoping that it all ends well without the safety of others being compromised. My phone was ringing off the hook with family and friends calling to ensure that I was safe. The four well-known senior student-athletes' names and faces were plastered all over national news. As an educator, this made me feel somewhat embarrassed because I worked on this campus. Being a mother myself, I felt very hurt and disappointed in the students' actions.

I would have never imagined in my wildest dreams they would have robbed a Game Stop store and ran back onto the school campus. Were these the same seniors at prom standing on the stage, making it rain by throwing money on the floor? Of course, that was shut down immediately. I would have named several other students before ever placing these young men at the scene. I had a good relationship with one of them, who was known as a hothead, but he allowed his mouth to place him in situations he could have easily avoided. Despite his smart mouth, he was a very prideful young man who had never been in any major trouble on campus.

He was one of my favorite seniors; I had to watch him get handcuffed and lead out the auditorium by police on that day. I was like his second mother away from home on school grounds. His mom and I often discussed issues and concerns regarding his behavior and consequences because of his sarcastic mouth. She stood behind the campus a hundred and ten percent when his behavior was not justified. She believed in the concept of "it takes a village to raise a child." So, how could this happen?

Even though I was very disappointed in his actions, I could not give up on him. Can you believe he even used his girlfriend to call me from jail? He was always apologetic for his actions and promising to do better. It was as if he needed my forgiveness, and I was very willing to grant it to him. More importantly, for me, he knew Mrs. Taylor still cared about his well-being and future, so I was not going to give up on him. I wanted to show him I was willing to stand by him as if he was my own son, even though he made a poor decision. It was a pivotal movement for him as he was trying to figure out who still believed in him, who had given up on him, and who he had left as a support system? Besides, he was getting ready to face one of the biggest battles of his life - his future.

The positive relationship I established with the student allowed him to feel comfortable and safe to want to reach out to me despite the wrong choices he made. The relationships between students and teachers play a large role in the trajectory of their academic success and social development. As educators, you understand students much better when you have a rapport, and trust is necessary for that rapport to develop.

I wanted him to have the confidence and faith to know he can make it through despite the odds stacked up against him. I did not know I would need the same confidence to fight the issues I had brewing ahead.

"You have to fight through some bad days,
to earn the best days of your life."
~Kristi Kunselman

CHAPTER 2

I Am Not Taking the Blame

THE SUPERINTENDENT, HIS cabin, the Chief of Police for the district, and all of the administrators were called to an emergency meeting. Little did I know this meeting would change the course of my life as an educator.

Here we go! I knew the district was going to try to place the blame on someone, and I was hoping it was not the principal. He was a fairly new principal on campus and was not given full autonomy to make changes on the campus as he saw fit. The principal of the campus and all administrators were blamed for this incident. The Chief of Police response was that it should not have happened under any circumstances. He proceeded to act surprised as if he was hearing concerns of the safety issues on campus for the first time. He was fully aware of the possibilities of students being able to leave and come back on the school campus.

I sat there with everyone else in total disbelief! What? I was thinking, how could he even ask that question? He knew the safety issues we've had on campus for the last ten years. He was a part of the problem by not providing resources such as locks and alarms on doors, creation of safety plans, and many requests of more officers for the campus. Since the first day of school, the administrators had asked for an extra officer to monitor the outside of the campus because we had close to 3,000 students with only two police officers and were known for violence. The disciplinary issues were always negative in the public eye of the media.

The district failed to get metal detectors until a stabbing account at one of the oldest and most prestigious high schools in the district. The Head of Schools Officer began to chime in on the meeting and attempted to reprimand the administrators about how she was displeased with the hallway and the campus when she visits. Really? This is what you choose to do at our most shocking moment! It made the team feel like we were responsible for the students choosing to make poor choices and put the entire campus in danger. The district completely missed the point that students and staff did not feel safe on campus prior to this incident.

She went on to state the campus leadership team was not doing enough and not visible in the hallway. The same people denied students we recommended for Disciplinary Alternative Education Placement (DAEP) that had a history of causing disruptions on campus. Yet, the Superintendent cabin placed and approved students with ankle bracelets and students straight out of the juvenile facility to be enrolled on the campus. Even when the school principal would deny the students for the safety of our campus, his superiors would overwrite his decision. I could not believe the blame that was being placed on us! They were fully aware of the safety issues and problems on this campus for years but failed to do anything about it.

"I blame myself for expecting more than
I should have out of you."
~ Unknown

CHAPTER 3

Fighting Educational Politics with Confidence

I COULD NOT BELIEVE what I was hearing, nor could I sit there and allow these people to beat us down worse than we already felt from the events of today. For most of us, it was truly the worst day of our career. How could they blame us for safety issues that were absolutely beyond our control? Why was the district refusing to take ownership of these issues? Some of the leadership cabin knew I was one of the advocates for campus safety. This was because of incidents I had not only been involved with, but also witnessed, and experienced in the past. I was one of the employees with the longest tenure and was working on the campus a year after it was established. So, trust me when I say I have seen quite a bit.

The moment of truth had arisen! Was I just going to sit there in silence or speak out? I mean, no one else was saying anything, so who am I to speak the truth? Confidence is sometimes the motivation we need when things get tough. Confidence is as important to leadership as oxygen is to breathing. If you are lacking in confidence, we are lacking in influence (Lolly 2019). It was time to practice what I had been preaching.

That is it! I could no longer sit in silence. I reminded the Chief of Police of the district and the Head of Schools that the leadership team offered several solutions and proposed plans to attempt to make the campus safer, but somehow, the plans never seemed to manifest. I reiterated how it does not help when students are being placed on the campus that have criminal records, are sex offenders, and wear ankle monitors as well. It is intimidating for other students to see in the classroom. When I say "placed," I mean the students were denied entry by the principal, but the decision to admit was overridden by the Superintendent cabin.

At that moment, I chose to fight for my students and myself. I decided a long time ago that I would not compromise my integrity once I was in a leadership position. The parents have trusted me to adhere to my professional responsibilities, be fair, and do what is best for their children, and I plan to honor and do exactly that. My educational philosophy is simple, "Do what's best for the kids." Somehow, the district forgot about what is best for the students and began doing what was best for them, the image of the school district, and funding.

Throughout my life, I have always been a confident person. However, I knew confidence and grit would be the two defining factors that would help determine the future ahead. Do I have what it takes to speak out alone? Is it that important to keep my integrity? The questions of self-doubt began to surface in my mind.

It is not a surprise to me that in my ten years of experience, my relationship with most of my students was built around having to discipline them. Most of them were not amused with me, nor did they like me upon our initial introduction meeting. It was not until later they learned to respect and love me because of the relationship and bond that was built. My student relationships were built off trust and fairness. Educators understand the importance of building a relationship with students. When teachers take the time to build a stronger relationship with their students, it creates a stronger understanding of what individual students need to achieve higher levels of growth. We must get to know our students on different levels, not just academically but socially as well. You may have the academic knowledge to teach them, but they can care less until they know you care about them as a person.

Building relationships with students is by far the most important thing a teacher can do. Without a solid foundation and relationships built on trust and respect, no quality learning will happen. While I believe the importance of relationships cannot be overstated, many teachers have no idea where to start. This is especially true when attempting to build relationships with students who come from a different background than you do (Ferlazzo 2018).

Students will do almost anything for you when they know you genuinely care about their well-being. Students tend to love very hard. Unbelievably, I have literally had to stop students from going after adults and other students they have witnessed being disrespectful towards me. That is how strong the bond can be. My students trust that I have their best interests at heart and confide in me with many issues because they trust I will protect and take care of them. Also, they trust me with their safety to come together to mediate a situation and be fair with disciplinary consequences. What is the cliché saying, "Students don't care how much you know until they know how much you care?"

I could not fully comprehend what happened to doing what is best for the kids? We are in the business of serving all children, so why does politics sit front and center over issues? I know some educators in higher leadership may argue that it is not that simple. Why not? I am aware that schools must get funding, and districts must abide by guidelines to keep the funding, but we must also keep our integrity and remember we have human lives at stake that are depending on adults to make the right decisions in their best interest. We are their models!

> *"In politics, nothing happens by accident.*
> *If it happens, you can*
> *bet it was planned that way."*
> *~Franklin D. Roosevelt*

CHAPTER 4

Where There Is Fear, Faith Cannot Exist

WAS I GOING to resign on my own or trust God in this situation? Well, I decided to trust God and hire an attorney. In this exact moment, my career changed in a way that I would have never known. Five months later, little did I know, I would endure a series of "retaliation" events that would force me to resign after ten years of service on the campus and as the Assistant Principal. It made an astounding effect on me because it changed my life and the way I viewed education forever, which truly tested my faith. The terms of my resignation were blamed on the fact that I was operating on a principal's probationary certificate, which is indeed legal in Texas.

The Texas Education Code states, "an intern or probationary certificate may be issued to a candidate for a certification class other than a classroom teacher who meets the requirements and conditions, including the subject matter knowledge requirement, prescribed in 230.37 (i) A candidate for an intern or probationary certificate class other than classroom teacher must meet all requirements established by the recommending EPP, which shall be based on the qualifications and requirements for the class of certification sought and the duties to be performed by the holder of a probationary certificate in that class."

This law allows aspiring school principals to work in the position as an Assistant Principal on a probationary certificate before obtaining a standard certificate. You can only work in a position as a principal on a probationary certificate for two years, and the Texas Education Agency has to approve it before you can accept an Assistant Principal position.

Faith without works is dead! So, I put all my trust in God and hired an attorney. All the devotions, prayers, and meditating I completed on faith, began to play repeatedly in my head. Are you going to just talk about your spiritual journey, or will you live it? The self-doubt I was experiencing had to be leveraged into confidence. I had to focus on what I knew and put all self-doubt aside. The key was to focus on my competency and capabilities, so I could find the confidence I needed to press through.

As an Assistant Principal of a high school campus, my day would start as early as 6:30 a.m. I am not a morning person but have been groomed to be due to my profession. However, I knew how important it was that I found meditation and devotion time before beginning my workday. I had to ensure I was in the proper mindset to deal with teenagers on a campus that operates in a fast-paced and requires quick problem-solving skills. For example, a multitude of teachers not showing up for work on a daily basis was a consistent issue.

My early morning devotions were about putting on the full armor of God and how His grace is sufficient. Every year, I have a devotional book that I choose to focus on, and this particular year I adopted Priscilla Shirer's *Put on the Full Armor of God* devotional book. I would read and work through the book at night or on the weekends when I had additional time.

Looking back on the year of 2018, as I revisited that devotional book, it became clear to me that God was preparing me for this exact situation. I even found a prayer I had written that matched exactly what I was going through perfectly. Then it dawned on me. I asked for this! You may ask, "What?" Yes, I did indeed ask for this!

Have you ever experienced continuing to work on a job knowing it was time for you to leave? Certain events may have confirmed the time for your departure, but you ignored them. It happens to all of us when a greater calling is in store somewhere else. I often talk with a very close friend and express how I feel like I should be doing something greater, affecting and serving more people. We also have an ongoing inside joke that, "When everybody starts getting stupid, it is time to go." Lol!

Let me explain. When we start feeling like we are the smartest person in the room and everybody else is not thinking it is our signal that we have no more room to grow and are no longer being challenged, so it is time to branch off to the next adventure of our career. I was never sure of what that would entail or even how to go about achieving "greater" or influencing more people in the educational field. Nor had God given me a sign of where to start, until now!

Leaving my position abruptly caused speculation and rumors to begin to surface. Phone calls and text messages began to pour in curious of how long I would be out. I was still answering questions from my secretary, as people on the job began to fill in on my duties and responsibilities in my absence, thinking I would return soon. Anxiety, worry, anger, disbelief, and other emotions set in. Not to mention all the questions that come with losing a job. What about bills? I have a kid in college, etc... My God had already planned it out and had wonderful things in store while I was going through this madness. The ultimate question he posed to me was, "Are you going to be transparent and share your story?" On the other hand, "Would I remain embarrassed and hide?" "Are you willing to share your story with strangers, or will you pick and choose who you want to share it with?"

After I got over the shock of it all and realized this was supposed to happen and nothing I could have done would have avoided this humiliation. I began to have a sense of peace about what I was going through, and my mindset shifted as I began to focus on what it is the Lord wanted me to do. One thing I knew for sure is, He did not bring me this far to leave me!

"Faith consists in believing when it
is beyond the power of reason."
~ Voltair

CHAPTER 5

Resilience: Check Your Mindset

AFTER LOSING MY job due to working on a state approved probationary principals certificate, I was on a mission. I had something to not only prove to myself but to others who wished for my downfall. I was determined to pass the principal's exam this last time around. Besides, I had taken it twelve times already. Geesh!

My emotions and mindset were in a battle that already had a proven record of failure and doubt in it. I was already disappointed in myself and felt some type of way about not being able to pass this exam. I mean, I was already a principal for God's sakes! Lord, why would you give me this job if this were not my path or your will? I made a daily commitment to keep a positive mindset after all of these unfortunate events.

Sometimes our circumstances can cause one to have doubt in yourself and God. Oh, but when I reflect back on how I started in the field of education (that too is another testimony), I refuse to believe he would let me drown. I had something to prove! I studied for hours, daily.

My daily routine began with early morning devotion; time with God always put me in a good positive headspace. I would listen to Tony Evans, Charles Stanley through their app on my phone or do interactive devotions with Priscilla Shirer's devotional book. Then, I would head to my favorite coffee shop, Starbucks, to study for hours at a time. Next, I would go workout because it always seemed to clear my mind, relieve stress, and give me the confidence to keep going. Finally, I would make it back home to prepare dinner for my hubby.

Did I have grit? Did I have what it took to continue in the field of education or even the courage to move forward? Grit is passion plus perseverance with a growth mindset. It is the defining factor, which allows people to succeed during the most challenging circumstances and life altering events. Will the self-doubt over power my thoughts to accept this was the reality of the situation? I was no longer going to be able to do what I love. The growth mindset I already established gave me the confidence to believe this problem was only temporary. I would tell myself I needed to stop mourning and continue to persevere after the career you worked so hard to obtain.

It is important that you have a consistent routine of ways you affirm yourself every day and remain in constant communication with God when you are in a place of doubt. It was my repeated routine for months and then it happened! I finally passed the principal exam! Whoo hooo! I was so excited! I had finally overcome a huge cloud I felt was over my head. More importantly, I triumphed the doubt that tried to stay embedded in my mind, and I ceased the moment! I realized what I was going through was defining moments that would affect the rest of my life, whether I succeeded or not. I had to give it my all and then I would be able to accept whatever the outcome.

Lord, you sure have a sense of humor! Lol! Everything I had was tested, as well as what I stood for as a woman. The Lord was testing my faith, my trust, who I thought I was, my confidence, my strength, persistence, and my spirituality. I am the optimistic friend who encourages everyone else but thank God for my friends, peers, and associates that genuinely loved me and returned the favor. God knew whom to call on to send me a message. I am forever grateful to you all, for obeying God when He guided you to check on me, send me a text message, or words of encouragement.

"Resilience is all about being able to overcome the unexpected."
~Jamais Cascio

CHAPTER 6

How to Bounce Back!

What? I asked for this.

MY PRAYER SIX months prior..."Lord, I am thankful for my life, marriage, and family. I am grateful for what you are going to do in my life and career. Please forgive me for resisting you in any part of my life. You have shown me repeatedly to trust that you will work it out for my good. I am asking that I take the principal exam for the last time this year and pass it. It has been a hard journey not knowing if I will be able to remain in my position as an Assistant Principal. My peers and coworkers know I have something special in me and for that, some want to see me fail. I want to show you, in all that I do! I want to give you all the glory! I know you are an intentional God and your moves are strategic and calculated in my life. I say, "Yes" and trust what you have for me."

My breakthrough came when I realized I asked for what had occurred in my career. I know you are confused right. When I stated in my prayer, "Please forgive me for resisting you in my past when you have shown me over and over again to trust you. I say "yes" and trust what you have is only made for me." I begin to ask for forgiveness and totally surrender all my plans to Him.

One day, I was having a tough day and needed a word so, I went back through my devotional book and found this prayer. It was seeing

17

this prayer that gave me the confidence to move forward; wondering is this my breakthrough to move to the next level? As previously stated, I knew I should be doing more, serving and impacting more lives, I just did not know how.

Honestly, I wanted the elevation in my career and life but was scared of the change. Like most of us are if we are honest with ourselves, we do not want our world to be disrupted by anything out of the ordinary. Especially, if we are content in our lives and things seem to be going well. See, when God is trying to take you to another level, He will shake up your world a little bit, maybe even turn it upside down to get your attention and make you uncomfortable. You cannot level up and stay still! It just does not work that way!

I have always desired to be successful. Many years ago, I learned that it needed to be success God's way for me to truly enjoy life. I never wanted to be famous or popular, but I have always aspired to be successful in everything that I do. As I grew spiritually, I realized success to the world and to God has two different meanings. God's definition of success is often different from ours.

Godly success does not depend on how many possessions we have, but on how few possessions we need to be content in life, and thus, in our willingness to joyfully share our abundance with others. It is how we ascetically strive without ceasing to sacrifice for others and to bless the lives of others. The worlds meaning of success is the total opposite. It is measured by how much money we have and how many possessions we can acquire.

He wants us to succeed in our obedience and faithfulness to Him through His word and in our development of Christ-like character (Joshua 1:8). Obedience is hard! I cannot find any passage where Moses gladly stepped up to serve, but he did it anyway, even though it was difficult. Many times, I had to do this as a leader in education. We have to remember our experiences are not just about us. It is because of our experiences we can walk someone else through the path, be vulnerable, open about how we felt, and be transparent by sharing and showing them how we made it through.

So, be careful what you pray for! If I didn't write that prayer down, I would have still been wondering why this happened to me or what lesson I was supposed to learn from it. I feel it is important for one to journal their prayers. It is strange to say, but I almost felt relieved. I prayed to go to the next level in my career. However, as an Assistant Principal at the time, I never desired to lead a school or become a head principal. Yet, I never explored any other opportunities that could be out there. I was always focused and determined on passing the principal's exam.

Learning to be flexible, honest, and humble about one's limitations is important. We may not always know what is best, but we need to be less obstinate concerning our prayer requests and more trusting because God may have a different path or some creative means to accomplish His will in our lives. I know this probably makes you nervous and even cringe if you are honest with yourself.

Trust me! I know this is cliché, but He has never failed me yet. When God places or changes something in my life that I do not like, it always benefits me in some way because He always teaches me new things about myself. For instance, I was propelled to step out of my comfort zone and work with people I otherwise would have never worked with or even talked to on my own.

God truly has a sense of humor! I have found myself working with people I would have never collaborated with by choice. I truly look up and laugh because he knows I am picky about who gets close to me. I do not play about my circle of people! Okay! Besides, I never desired to be a teacher. Now, look at God!

"My setbacks may have amused you,
but my comebacks are going to confuse you."
~Sue Ekins

PART II

Practical Advice for Students

CHAPTER 7

Why Confidence and Knowledge Depends on Your Success?

FOR MOST STUDENTS, confidence is a natural personality trait: Either you have it, or you don't. If you don't have it, you should begin to build it as quickly as possible because in doing so, you safeguard one of the most important ingredients to success: motivation. Confidence is vital to a student's success. The amount of confidence you possess will affect many aspects of your goals. Self-confidence is something you create in your mind.

Four Ways to Build Confidence:

1. Learn how to positively cope with any mistakes and failures. It is a good thing to view failure as a learning experience. You must fail in order to succeed.

2. You must learn to love yourself. Re-evaluate the standards you hold. Re-learn your priorities and set new standards based off of your principles and beliefs.

3. Start small. Start taking a few small risks to overcome some of your fears. Do something that scares you.

4. Get the knowledge and get out of your own way. Acknowledge your weaknesses and seek support. Invest energy in it and work hard at it to sharpen that skill.

To grow in a career, gaining as much knowledge as possible is important because without knowledge, one cannot be successful in life. Also, you must wholeheartedly fight to gain as much knowledge as possible to aid in your interactions with others.

When you pursue knowledge, you equip yourself with practical skills and the necessary tools to apply in the workplace. The information you gain is not just interesting to know but will be of great use to you in your current role and the future ahead.

Education and confidence are very important to your success in life. As education and learning are constantly evolving, knowledge can be obtained in a variety of ways. Attempting to cater to how students learn is a constant learning process for educators. New research is constantly testing new ideas and theories to assist with student learning such as mindfulness being an intricate part in the classroom. The professional development offered each year is filled with new ideas for Teachers to support students in the classroom. The Millennials and Generation X did not buy into the philosophy that education can only be obtained inside the four walls of a classroom on a school campus. They have expanded their resources on how to get educated to be successful in life. They are actually thinking outside the box and using critical thinking to use the biggest media outlet in the world to get educated such as Facebook, Instagram, and Twitter.

Today, a whopping two billion people are active on Facebook at least once a month, which is almost a third of the world's population. LinkedIn has over 500 million members. Twitter has over 320 million users daily. Add to this the number of people using YouTube, Instagram, Pinterest, Google+, Kickstarter, and other Social Media platforms, and it's easy to see why they have become the go-to for 21st century entrepreneurs. The platforms are making young people more entrepreneurial than ever.

So, no matter how you gain it. Education gives us knowledge of the world around us and changes it into something better. It helps us to develop a certain perspective of how we view and form opinions of life.

It truly is the key to success because without a good education, or a healthy dose of common sense, you will find it hard to achieve success. A good education is important because you will be able to think for yourself and communicate intelligently to other people.

Knowledge and education can increase productivity, collaboration, and social engagement, which have far-reaching effects. It empowers you to do a job faster and more efficiently, which will benefit you well in your career.

The knowledge we pose is what sets us apart from our peers and our competition. The skills we pose and how we deliver them is what makes us unique in a way that we can get results and get the job done.

What are you doing with the knowledge that you have? Are you being a good steward? Are you willing to share that knowledge to empower others? How does the knowledge you possess benefit you?

The confidence a student possesses is as vital as the knowledge they obtain. The amount of confidence they possess will affect their education and life goals. When you are starting your professional life, you must have confidence in your abilities because you have not proven them yet.

Self-confidence is influenced by factors such as your upbringing, work environment, and level of dedication when pursuing a cause.

Here are 6 Mental Ways to Build Self Confidence:

1. Stop comparing yourself to others.
2. Embrace self-doubt.
3. Try telling your brain "NO!"
4. Visualize yourself as you want to be.
5. Affirm yourself. Think positive to overcome negative bias.
6. Face your fears. Do something that scares you.

Practicing these simple routines can change your life. Self-confidence is an umbrella term for knowing how to have resilience, emotional restraint, and relationships. It all feeds into creating a personality of confidence.

The time is now for you to take control of your future and gain the knowledge and confidence needed to be successful. What you are doing now is training yourself on how to move forward for the rest of your life. I challenge you to take control of your life and build your confidence.

"Confidence comes naturally with success.
But, success comes only to those who are confident."
~Unknown

PART III

Practical Advice for Teachers

CHAPTER 8

Safety First! Let's Be Proactive, NOT Retroactive in the Classroom

AS I HAVE lived out one of the most life-changing days I had in education, it made me face my worst fear of safety violations while working on a school campus. Was I prepared to know what to do if an intruder or school shooter entered the campus? The school district definitely did not prepare me or anyone else on campus for that matter. If safety was a serious concern, for me and millions of other educators, why did I waste time waiting on the school district to prepare me for my worst day on a school campus? When reflecting back on how I felt the moment the police entered the campus with weapons drawn, I knew I was going to take control of my own professional development needs and seek the help I needed to feel safe at work.

The truth is some districts focus on professional development more than others. Some have targeted training not just on the district needs, but the campus needs as well. With retention rates high in the education field, districts have experienced wasting funds training individuals one year, only to have to train someone else the next year due to them leaving the profession. With the increase in school shootings, why aren't the schools taking control and being proactive in the training development? Perhaps another solution would be for districts to include more safety trainings yearly and have mandatory updates that staff must attend.

Career development is my choice. Do I choose to invest in my career or not? If I were not willing to invest in me, then why would I expect someone else to do so? The purpose of career development is to enhance each employee's current job performance. Teachers tend not to take ownership of this area of improving their career and sharpening classroom skills. From my experience, those teachers that do not, often times are not very good at what they do, which makes them low performing teachers who produce low performing students. Also, it shows they are not committed and invested in making a difference in students' lives. Sadly, it's because they don't think they can enhance their skills.

As most educators are lifelong learners, I was guilty of not investing in my own professional development needs. I have never taken my safety on campus seriously enough to invest in it with my own funds outside of the school district.

I have always been an advocate for campus safety and pushed for more training for staff members. I was able to make a little progress with the district police officers to do a mini-training for an active shooter. Unfortunately, the training was not mandatory, which means most staff members were not present, and it did not occur during the start of the year for the purpose of preparation. I do commend the district police department for a good interactive training that started the conversation around the importance of safety on campus.

Make no mistake, safety has always been a number one concern for me, especially with the recent school shootings. The incident I experienced was definitely scary and a revelation in many ways. Was our campus prepared for a tragic event? Did teachers know what to do in case things went bad? Were staff and students fully aware of the emergency plan? My honest answer, "No!"

The district nor the campus had ever taken the safety of students and staff seriously, in my opinion. How did I come to this conclusion? I came to this conclusion from things I have witnessed and my own experiences on the campus. Unfortunately, I even had a parent enter the campus to confront me about something her son did in class while I was on hall duty in between class changes. Students that did not attend the school often times were caught on campus trying to fight other students. Not to mention, the weapons and brawls that occurred on campus between African-American and Hispanic students.

Do these things happen on other high school campuses? Yes. Unfortunately, this high school was not in good graces with the media because negative incidents were always exposed to the public. Even though I know other high school campuses had similar issues, I would also see those districts trying to make immediate changes because they understood the safety risk. Students cannot learn if they do not feel safe, nor are teachers able to teach in the classroom. Maslow's hierarchy of needs for teachers and students provides a framework that students and teachers are less likely to perform at their full potential if their basic needs are unmet. Educators have always looked at Maslow's hierarchy of needs with students in mind but not for teachers. Maslow's theory says that the need to feel safe must be satisfied before individuals higher needs are met.

Teachers selflessly give to their students in order to meet their needs. The sacrifices they make are unlimited because they only want the best for their students. Teachers are too busy being the person young people need to be successful. The truth is not only should students feel secure and safe, but so should the adults if we want them to perform at their full potential for students.

Teachers want the professional development that supports an ongoing culture of safety in schools—as they are under more pressure than ever. School violence in the U.S. has become a cultural maelstrom, and two groups—teachers and students—stand in the eye of the storm, in dire need of our active support. In a March 2018 survey, when teachers were asked what they want when it came to violence prevention, the response was resoundingly ongoing professional development would help them proactively support at-risk and troubled students day-to-day. Ninety-three percent of teachers stated that they want this kind of development on an ongoing basis. It was reported that less than half of them have received it. In addition, a third report their schools do not offer the professional development at all. However, every teacher deserves professional development—in the form of practical and substantive training—so they can safely and confidently focus on teaching. Every student deserves the benefits of a safe and productive learning environment (Crisis Prevention Institute 2019).

I know what you are thinking, at the beginning of the year, every district is responsible and held accountable for providing professional development on safety. Yes, we were trained on fire drills as well as what to do when the campus goes on lockdown. Lockdown is when no one can move throughout the building during that time. However, we never completed an active intruder training, which is at the top of the list of topics for school safety.

Considering the horrific school shootings in the news over the last two decades, the events that have already occurred on campus and in the district truly showed me over the years the district did not value the importance of safety. It was not until a student's death at the sister High School from a violent attack that the district allowed metal detectors to be used when entering the school campus.

Why did a precious life need to be sacrificed to realize the state of the district? The most disturbing fact about the entire situation is that the high school campuses were already in possession of metal detectors but only allowed to use them at athletic events. The gut-wrenching feeling will never subside of how a student's life could have possibly been saved by being proactive with taking safety precautions. When I asked about using metal detectors prior to this tragic event, it was explained to me with a clear and concise tone of how the image of the district was more important than the lives of students and staff.

According to Campus Safety Magazine, the statistics are as follows:

K-12 School Shooting Statistics

- There have been 1,300 school shooting incidents since 1970.

- 2018 had the greatest number of school shooting incidents since 1970, with 82-recorded incidents.

- 2018 was the highest year for the number of victims killed, including the shooter, with 51 killed.

- California, Texas, and Florida are the top three states in the U.S. with the most (school shooting) incidents.

- 669 incidents occurred outside on school property, and 588 occurred inside the school building.

- Most school shootings occurred in the morning.

This was my ah-ha moment! I realized as a staff member, I had to take safety in my own hands if I was going to continue to work in education and especially on that particular school campus. I began to focus more on-campus safety and spoke with Spring ISD Police about more training. Also, I began to make plans in advance for my own safety. What preventative measures can I take on campus if the unthinkable happened? I began to ask myself these simple questions:

1. Where is the best hiding place in the school?

2. What would I do if students and I were stuck in a classroom?

3. What was the quickest way to get out of the building?

These questions may seem minor, but I would not want to have to make these decisions in a moment of fear and panic. Since teachers and students are the majority on a school campus, it was then I realized teachers must take safety into their own hands to protect themselves and students.

Teachers should have their own plan of safety in the classrooms. As teachers, there are things we can do every day in our classrooms to begin to prepare our students for a tragic situation. It is the simple but important things that some of us are already doing, which coincide with good classroom management. What is it you may ask? Good habits and routines not only help to keep a classroom organized and managed but can also save your life. One simple example, I trained my students every year to keep the classroom door closed and locked during instruction. If someone came to the door, they knew to get my permission from me to open it first, which added a layer of resistance.

A layer of resistance provides the assailant fewer opportunities to complete their mission. If layers of resistance are present, it creates time to be controlled in favor of the victims.

It is an effective measure because it provides fewer opportunities for an assailant to complete their mission. Here are a few tips on how to create layers of resistance in the classroom:

1. Active team building. It develops communication and increases the success of the team. All parties know and understand their role in a situation.

2. Provide classroom routines and consistency.

3. Doors should be locked during instructional time.

4. Teach the class how to shield themselves, hide, and barricade doors effectively.

5. Help students support each other. Peer learning is a great best practice that students benefit from greatly. Learning from each other on how to respond to difficult situations is another layer of support for students.

6. Have classroom non-negotiables. Classroom non-negotiables is an expectation that must occur in the classroom such as being respectful to all students that enter the classroom.

The layers of resistance will help to defend their area while protecting students. We must not wait and depend on the district to protect us. We must protect ourselves.

Effective teacher professional development is a way for teachers to invest in their careers while taking responsibility for their career needs. It provides relevant training to developing teachers that will enhance their job performance. Safety was important to me at that time.

What is important for you to be better and more effective in your career in education with students? Recent research indicates that certain characteristics of professional development are related to effectiveness in changing teacher practice and improving student learning. In particular, professional development has been found to be most effective when it focuses on the content of the subject taught and corresponds with school or classroom activities. It provides active learning opportunities that is sustained over time that involves collective participation of teachers from the same school, subject, or grade and includes administrative support for planning and implementing change (Darling-Hammond et al. 2009; Desimone 2009; Desimone and Garet 2015; Whitworth and Chiu 2015; Yoon et al. 2007). In my own research, I could have been more mentally prepared on that day of such a life-altering event. It was important to have the right frame of mind to focus on and remain calm for students had the situation ended another way.

In addition, some school districts do not take preventative measures to keep students and staff safe. It is not until after a horrific event occurs and the media shines an ugly light on the situation, which causes multiple questions that now have to be answered. What was done to prevent this situation from occurring? How was it able to happen? As these questions are answered, many more will follow. When it comes to school safety, this country is known to be retroactive. We react after the incident has occurred. We do not want to think about students doing the unthinkable on a school campus, but we live in a day and age where we must. Consider how far behind we will be if we are so afraid to take a stand and create change in schools. Most importantly, failure to do so will cause more innocent children's lives to be lost.

A proactive approach focuses on eliminating problems before they have a chance to appear, and a reactive approach is based on responding to events after they have happened. The difference between these two approaches is the perspective each one provides in assessing actions and events.

Metal detectors, security resource officers, and I.D. badges are some of the traditional preventative methods used to curb violence. The reactive measures may indeed reduce or prevent weapons from being used in schools, but a much broader, more proactive approach seems to be needed if violence is to be curbed for the long term. "Schools that impose order, rather than cultivating it, may win no more than an uneasy truce while at the same time losing the hearts and minds of their students" (Gaddy 1987, pp. 28 - 29). The act of working on building a culture and a respective learning environment could ultimately be the long-time proactive answer to limiting violence in school.

Safety first! It is the golden rule you learn when you become a teacher, especially an administrator. However, often time's safety is not what we see placed as a priority in districts. The experience taught me that it is my responsibility to get the professional development needed to ensure my own safety and professional needs are met.

Professional development is accessible in a variety of ways such as online courses, webinars, etc...We have no excuse! I am guilty too! After many years in education, instead of me prioritizing my own safety and career needs, I was waiting on the district to provide professional development I felt was very important - safety. The expectation is that we will be provided with the necessary tools we need as teachers and educators to be successful inside the classroom while on campus. However, the reality is that it is ultimately our responsibility to get the professional help and support we need.

I discovered the hard way that is the wrong attitude to have as a professional. It is by the grace of God no one has ever been seriously injured on that campus. The truth is, it is my professional responsibility to perfect my craft, to get professional development where I need it, and to grow with my career field. You are the only one that knows what is needed to feel more confident and help you perform your best at your craft. Education consistently evolves and so should we.

Students must feel safe in order to learn. Teachers must feel safe to perform at their best. What is the benefit to ensuring you take professional development in your own hands? It just may save your life! I will continue to express, it is our professional responsibility to seek what you need for your career and safety. It is not just the responsibility of the school districts.

Finally, not only will you be prepared for an emergency, you will feel more confident in the classroom. A confident teacher makes for confident learners allowing room for academic success.

You cannot choose to wait on someone else to make you feel safe while working on a school campus. Alternatively, you can choose to protect yourself and make sure you are prepared in case of a crisis. If a school crisis were to occur on your campus right now, would you be prepared? What professional development training have you taken this year? Have you invested in yourself this year?

"Too many professional development
initiatives are done to teachers –
not for, with, or by them."
~Andy Hargreaves

PART IV

Practical Advice for Administrators

CHAPTER 9

More than Laborers (Teachers Are Workers)

L ET US BE honest with ourselves on the topic – "Education is a job of serving." We are indeed workers! We do a unique work in special ways that require specific skills. Sometimes educators lose sight of that by getting caught up in all the fancy titles that come along with climbing the education career ladder. Have you ever met anyone that has climbed the glorious mountain of degrees? They make it to the top and are awarded their Doctoral degrees. What a great accomplishment, right? Now from this point forward they can no longer be called by their name without Dr. being in front of it. Lol! I do not have my doctoral degree, but I get it. You earned it, so you should be respected. However, let us not let that shift the focus of the reason you went back to school to get a doctoral degree. It was to change lives, and make a difference with students and that should be the sole and only reason. For me, obtaining a doctorate degree in education shows you are not afraid to take risks to try new innovative ways to reach students and improve the world of education for both teachers and students.

Teachers, counselors, and administrators, fundamentally, are relationship builders and, we do not need the distraction of thinking about prestige and titles. We perform the services of social workers, mental health counselors, police officers, nurses, and paramedics, which duties require verbal acuity, book smarts, and hard-earned lessons from the school of hard knocks.

We are "service professionals." Research shows the work we identify with most strongly is with workers. "Mehta argues that data-driven reform has again mandated discredited policies because respected professions "colonize" less respected professions. Since teachers are just a "semi-profession," outsiders feel entitled to micromanage us without paying attention to education research and history, or our professional judgments. The way to break out of this destructive cycle, says Mehta, is to upgrade our standards and become a full-fledged and respected profession." (Jal Mehta *The Allure of Order")* It is evident this would require teachers to look at themselves as professionals and not just service workers to get to the next level.

Teaching is an act of love and passion. It is a love and passion that cannot be accurately measured and rewarded by the elites. Teaching should be a team effort. "Professional" educators are no more worthy than bus drivers, lunchroom workers, and other mentors who help children grow into educated, healthy, responsible adults. Perhaps, our actions can change the way that some of the elites behave, and maybe even how they feel towards us.

In all, the protests occurring across the world regarding teacher's wages, it looks like we may have finally taken a stand. We are demanding to be paid for the many hats we wear as workers. Why should our titles matter in the team effort known as teaching and learning? Ask yourself - Are you more concerned with the job titles or the service it provides? Do you understand the importance and responsibility that comes with the title of being an "Educator"?

> *"Those who can, teach. Those*
> *who can't, pass laws about teaching."*
> *~Paul L. Jalbert*

CHAPTER 10

Teachers Need More Support!

TEACHERS ARE LEAVING the profession at an alarming rate. Ten percent of teachers will leave before finishing their first year in the classroom. In recent years, teacher retention has loomed large of the education reform debate. While there is no doubt, certain areas are affected by teacher shortages, primarily low-income and rural areas; there seems to be deeper problems at work—teacher retention. Statistics show low-income schools deal with much higher rates of turnover than affluent ones. According to Richard Ingersoll, a professor at the University of Pennsylvania's education school, 15 percent of teachers leave the profession every year and 40 percent of graduates with an undergraduate degree in education never use it (Public Agenda 2018). So, how do we keep effective teachers in the classroom where we so desperately need them? The effect on student outcomes is more difficult to quantify.

New teachers, who we know are more likely to quit, are assigned to low-income school districts at twice the rate they are assigned to high-income districts. They are also assigned to teach core subjects like math or reading with little or no training and assistance.

In order to keep effective teachers, we must first identify what causes teacher turn over. The rate of teacher turnover is caused by a number of factors in which three of the most cited reasons are lack of resources, salary, and no input. Low-income schools tend to suffer even more when teachers are not retained. In many cases, they are unable to keep veteran educators and thus need to hire new and inexperienced teachers every year. The Metlife Survey of American Teachers lists percentages of teachers who are likely not to stay in education. The percentage of teachers who say they are very likely to leave the profession has increased by 12 points since 2009, from 17% to 29%. (Metlife Survey of American Teachers 2011). The most cited reasons are:

1) Lack of Resources

Too often conversations about school funding are associated with demands to raise teachers' salaries, but the situation is far more complex. Many teachers, especially in urban schools, are working with at-risk students with very few of the necessary resources to support them in their education. Therefore, many teachers pay out of pocket for items needed for the classroom and the students. No teacher should have to worry about not being able to provide the most basic resources for their students. I do believe increased funding for high-quality resources, mental health services for at-risk students, and continued teacher development would absolutely improve urban education. Teachers in urban school areas are not equipped with the same level of resources as a teacher in a more affluent suburban area and/or school district. Often times, teachers in less fluent school districts teach with outdated books, not in the best condition, and with limited or no technology in the classroom. Teachers in affluent districts are not faced with those same issues, as they have a plethora of resources at their disposal. The playing field is not leveled for teachers or students, which could certainly affect academics.

2) Salary

In more than half the states, the average teacher is making below the living wage. Despite a relatively steady rise in per-pupil funding, real teacher salaries rose just 7 percent since 1970, and have been largely flat since 1990. Since the 2008 recession, per-pupil funding and real teacher salaries, both adjusted for inflation, have declined in most states.

This information is being reported during an era of teacher protests, demonstrations, and strikes largely centered on low wages. According to data from the National Education Association, the 2016-17 average public school teacher salary was $59,660, but that amount varied widely between states. While teachers in New York make a yearly average of $81,902, teachers in Mississippi make $42,925 on average—the lowest in the country. As labor market opportunities have improved outside of teaching, public schools have lost the captive labor pool they once had with respect to women (who make up over 75% of all kindergarten through 12th grade teachers) and are forced to compete with more lucrative professions for the best college graduates. The widespread desire in recent years to cut class sizes while simultaneously raising the quality of teachers (through such measures as No Child Left Behind) has made the recruiting task only that much more difficult. The concern over teacher quality has generated renewed interest in both the sufficiency of teacher pay to attract high-quality staff and the efficacy of various dimensions of teacher pay, including incentives and extra pay for working in particular fields or in particular locations (i.e., hard-to-staff schools) (Allegretto, Sylvia A, Sean P. Corcoran and Lawrence Mishel. *How Does Teacher Pay Compare? Methodological Challenges and Answers.* N.p.: Economic Policy Institute 2004).

We need to continue to launch conversations among state policymakers and district leaders on how to better use education funding. The first step should be allocating more money to education. Let us hope protests and strikeouts create long-term, substantial change, to meet the needs of our students. This will allow us to be able to contribute to improving the failing U.S. education system we are operating in today by exercising our right to go out and vote for those who will represent us locally and nationally. It will allow us to hold those in the proper position accountable for making differences our children can feel both in and outside of the classroom.

Ask yourself - What role are you playing on your school campus to help retain teachers? Are you a part of the solution or the problem? What creative and innovative ways have you used to get by in the classroom? How have you been able to survive with the lack of funds and resources provided to teachers? Forty-five percent of teachers are not satisfied with their salary.

Due to low pay, new teachers often cannot pay off their student loans or buy homes in the communities where they teach. Teachers and other certified educators often work two or three jobs to make ends meet. The stress and exhaustion can become unbearable – forcing people out of their vocation. In addition, harsh evaluation policies, worsening working conditions, and lack of professional support are pushing more teachers out of the profession. If school districts want their students to have the most professional teachers, they must pay a professional salary (National Education Association 2018).

3) No Input

Many teachers have reported they feel they have no say in decisions that ultimately affect their teaching. Teachers are not part of the conversations regarding school schedules, standardized testing, or in some cases even lesson planning. The lack of classroom autonomy is now one of the biggest sources of frustration for teachers nationally.

Harvard's Susan Moore-Johnson, director of The Project on the Next Generation of Teachers, found several key factors that influence teacher satisfaction: having ample time to collaborate during the school day, strong and supportive principals, and a common vision that is shared and executed by the school. Teachers need to feel included in decisions that affect their students' learning. They also need to be included in decisions that impact their day-to-day working conditions (Public Agenda 2018).

In supportive schools, teachers not only tend to stay, but they also improve at much greater rates over time. In a recent study, teachers were tracked in Charlotte-Mecklenburg Schools for up to ten years and examined how their individual effectiveness (as measured by contributions to student achievement) changed over time. It was found that teachers working in schools with strong professional environments improved, over ten years, 38% more than teachers in schools with weak professional environments did.

There were six measures drawn from teacher surveys to characterize the ideal environment: consistent order and discipline; opportunities for peer collaboration; supportive principal leadership; effective professional development; a school culture characterized by trust; and a fair teacher evaluation process providing meaningful feedback. Researchers from the University of Michigan and Vanderbilt have since used a similar research design to show how teachers in Miami-Dade County Public Schools improved at substantially faster rates in schools where effective collaboration takes place through instructional teams (Developing Work Places Were Teachers Stay, Improve, and Succeed 2015).

Across schools, teachers speak about specific supporting factors that facilitated their ability to succeed with students. They describe the value of establishing an orderly, disciplined learning environment, with student support services to attend to social and emotional needs, and efforts to engage parents. Furthermore, research suggests peer collaboration, feedback (from both peers and administrators), and instructional support can all be effective tools for building strong work environments and promoting teacher development.

It all comes down to collaboration as the key! In any thriving and performing organization, people want to feel comfortable with sharing their thoughts. They do not just want to help someone else achieve their goal and vision but want to know they play an intrigue part in helping the organization be successful. The staff will work harder to execute a goal if they have buy in and have contributed to the developing process.

From the Metlife Survey of American Teachers

- Slightly more than half (53%) of parents and two-thirds (65%) of teachers say public school teachers' salaries are **not** fair for the work they do.

- Teachers in schools with high parent engagement are more than twice as likely as those in schools with low parent engagement to say they are very satisfied with their job (57% vs. 25%).

- Parents in schools with high parent engagement are more likely than those in schools with low engagement to be optimistic student achievement will be better in five years (73% vs. 45%).

- Parents agree that they and their child's teachers work together to help their child succeed in school (96% vs. 55%).

- Rate other parents at their child's school as excellent or good in effectively engaging them in their child's school and education (82% vs. 21%).

National Center for Education – Profile of Teachers 2011

- 40% of teachers are not satisfied with the status of teachers in their community.

- One third (33 percent) of current public school teachers do not expect to be teaching in K-12 schools five years from now.

- Thirteen percent of current public school teachers expect to be retired five years from now.

- While 70 percent of white teachers and 57 percent of Hispanic teachers expect to be teaching K-12 levels five years from now, less than half (43 percent) of black teachers expect to be teaching K-12.

Many districts have announced raises for the upcoming 2019-2020 school year. However, some administrators and legislators still disregard the role professional compensation plays in recruitment in addition to retention, and minimize the complexities of teaching. In fact, according to the Learning Policy Institute, almost 20% of teachers leave the profession because of the low pay. Here are facts you can use to counter some of the falsehoods about teacher compensation.

Fiction: Teachers earn as much as comparable professionals for the work they do.

Fact: Over the past decade, the average classroom teacher salary has increased 15.2% but after adjusting for inflation, the average salary has actually decreased by $1,823 or 3.0%. The Economic Policy Institute (EPI) notes that comparable professionals with similar education earn higher salaries. Nationally, teachers earn 19% less than similarly skilled and educated professionals. This "teaching penalty" has increased significantly in the past 20 years – from approximately 2% in 1994 to 19% in 2017.

Fiction: Teaching is easy, so anyone can do it.

Fact: Teachers, like many professionals, including accountants and engineers, are trained, certified professionals as they have college degrees plus teaching credentials too. Also, many have advanced degrees and have completed extensive coursework in learning theory and educational practice. For most, teaching is a calling. However, the intrinsic rewards of an educational career should not be used as a rationale for low salaries.

"Teachers, I believe, are the most responsible and important members of society because their professional efforts affect the fate of the earth."
~Helen Caldicot

CONCLUSION: CHAPTER 11

Bold Her: All Things Work Together for Go(o)d

ONCE I DECIDED to have faith, overcome my fears, and be resilient in education, despite the hardship I was enduring - I regained confidence in my educational career and myself. Being confident about my strengths helped me to draw courage and resolution when the going got tough in my life. It helped me to keep things in perspective and back myself when the task ahead looked nearly impossible to complete in the stipulated time.

Self-confidence has always been instilled in me from my upbringing and family environment. However, it increases as you are dedicated towards pursuing a cause you believe in. In fact, going through this trial certainly raised my level of confidence. I knew I would have to step outside of my comfort zone to go to the next level in my career and continue to pursue my passion. I have gained a multitude of experience in my tenure as an educator. For instance, I have earned many titles such as "Director," "Assistant Principal," "Curriculum Writer," "Professional Developer," "Academy Leader," and many more. But I have to admit, just being a part of a team who opened up a new campus has exposed me to learning the ends and outs of what it takes to operate a functioning and successful school campus. Also, it taught me what a dysfunctional campus looks like as well. My on the job training was invaluable because it has given me tremendous knowledge of my educational philosophy, "do what's best for the kids."

So, what is next? I know there is more to the education field than just this. Where do I go from here? I began to think of ways I could be innovative in reclaiming my passion for education. I began to do research and take an interest in online businesses. It was fascinating to see the power of social media and the reach it had to all people. I ran across some amazing educators doing remarkable things and able to earn an income online. What impressed me the most was the impact they had on thousands of teachers and educators who were waiting and watching for them to drop the next best thing full of valuable and life-changing content. Then it dawned on me, this is how I will influence, impact, inspire and make a difference in education by being able to reach others all over the world. I began to spend endless hours learning how online businesses work, taking coaching classes, reading data on social media, and getting more technology savvy as to how it all works. I then discovered my passion for becoming an Edupreneur!

I am a true believer that everything works together for the good of those who love God, to those who are called according to His purpose (Romans 8:28). I had no choice but to leave my position after ten years. Nevertheless, I would not have known what an Edupreneur is nor that it existed at this day and age and thriving for many other like-minded people such as myself. Statistics show there has been a striking increase of online courses and eLearning in the last few years because people like to learn on their own time and in the comfort of their home. I am here for it! It is the concept of open learning.

Now, God has finally shown me how to use Education as a platform to get back into entrepreneurship, how to impact, the correct way to serve, and to use my gifts to do more of what he has purposed me to do. I am now learning how to be an Edupreneur. A year ago, I didn't even know the word existed. I never even heard of the word let alone knew what it actually entailed.

An Edupreneur lead with a 21st century mindset is known globally inside and outside of the classroom. It is someone who creates a positive value shift with the specific economic resource of "learning." The successful educator helps break down the boundaries. He or she opens up the movement of learning from one to many, from localized to global, from the past and present into the future - all while making a profit.

It allows me to be innovative and creative while focusing on educational value. I can be free to creatively allocate resources and support the education community, teachers, students, and parents without the strain of adhering to district policies and rules often attached. I am truly excited about that!

I am tasked to actively listen and honestly meet the needs of educators, to provide help, support, and resources. I have the freedom to motivate and coach teachers in a way I feel is successful by focusing on teacher confidence. My experience as an instructional coach has led me to witness when teachers are confident in their teaching capabilities, it increases academic success in the classroom with both student and teacher. The research confirmed what I experienced coaching teachers.

Confident teachers have a positive impact on his or her students' achievement, attitude, and even socio-emotional growth. To improve the schooling experience of low progress learners, enhancing teachers' beliefs in their teaching competence is a viable approach. Teacher efficacy is one of the few characteristics that can reliably predict students' learning outcomes. Teachers' beliefs in their teaching capabilities could affect how they perceive, approach, and teach their students (Singteach 2016).

A completely new world was revealed to me, one that required me to raise my self-confidence to pursue this career title. As an Edupreneur, it requires me to go LIVE on social media, engaging with people all over the world, making videos that thousands of people will see and judge. It rewards me with the freedom to teach what and how I would like and gain a profit.

A confident person is able to practice their skills and talents beyond expectations, has an opportunity to set goals, forget their own past mistakes, and learn new things. I am expanding my knowledge and engaging in 21st century learning and can be as creative as I would like.

Does this mean I will never go back to being a leader in public education? That would be a powerful statement to make. I truly enjoy working on a high school campus and in higher education; however, this opportunity affords me the space to use my passion freely to do what I love!

As stated previously, I knew my career working on a high school campus was not going to be the place where I retired. I understood I was only passing through in preparation for the future. Perhaps, at the moment, I was afraid of success elsewhere and was unable to visualize my future. I knew my success did not end there because we do not get to predict when God says move.

How bad do you want success? Do you want success God's way? Are you afraid of maximizing your potential? Are you afraid of what God may take you through to get there? The road will not be easy, and your life will be interrupted. It is scary, but it is all worth it. I am trusting His plan is so much better than mine and my gifts to discover my purpose.

We must always fight for what we believe in and what we are passionate about. Even when things don't always look the way we want them to and are not going according to our plan, we must trust the process! Think of the last time you refused to compromise and stood for what was right. How did it make you feel? How important is your integrity? Would you do it all over again?

By now, you understand where my passion from education comes from and why school safety is so important. Education is not just a job but also a calling for a special type of person with a love to work with young people.

We live in a different time where education is constantly evolving into the 21st century. We must quickly take heed and evolve with it, with not only 21st century learning but also how we view education if we want to reach millennial students.

The beauty of it all is this crossroad in my career caused me to challenge myself through my confidence, faith, integrity, and beliefs. Early in my career, I promised myself I would never sell out to politics. I would keep my integrity, spiritual beliefs, and values as I climbed the educational ladder. I was forced to prove it.

If you are passionate about education, and plan to stay in it for the long haul, take control of your future. Be open, free, and learn to adapt to this ever so changing field. Find a way to meet your professional development needs even if the school district is not changing fast enough to meet them. Sometimes it takes school districts awhile to catch up to student learning due to funding or simply just not willing to change at that time.

School districts tend to be retroactive and not proactive. Too many times, it takes something tragic to happen for their response to happen sooner. It should not be that way. I applaud districts that try to stay ahead of best practices and keep up with the current events involving safety.

We are no longer waiting on the district to meet our needs to be successful in education. It is about becoming a 21st century learner and making efforts to meet our own needs by seeking professional development and ensuring safety needs have been addressed.

Placing these issues in your control will build teacher efficacy that will give you the confidence you need to be successful in the classroom and create confident learners. Professional development tailored for your needs equals a confident teacher and learners who are more confident. Confident teachers can reach low performing students by giving them an entirely new experience in education.

I encourage you to do what God has purposed in your heart, despite the setbacks. Stay true to your purpose, passion, and vision for your life. Have **FAITH** that it will all work out for your good.

FEAR is what we must overcome when accomplishing our goals and purpose in life. Focus your mind on what is true in the midst of uncertain times. Embrace the beauty of not allowing fear and anxiety to control life. Take the initiative to seek what you need for yourself, including professional development to be confident in your career. I have the outlook now that every time I face my fears, something amazing happens!

Do you have grit? What is grit? Passion plus perseverance equals grit according to the research of Angela Ducksworth. You must have a growth mindset to be successful at life and know that you are worthy and capable of overcoming all challenges placed before you. The purpose in your heart eludes the mind to "Never Give Up" on your passion. "If you get tired, learn to rest, not quit."

To be **RESILIENT**, you must experience frustration, failure, and challenges. It comes from your beliefs and attitudes about yourself as well as your outlook on life. Keep your perspective, capture the opportunity, build competence, and encourage yourself daily. Remain confident about your strengths and teaching capabilities. Have a growth mindset and never give up!

Continuing on your journey takes confidence, determination, courage, and faith. It is the faith that once you have obtained your desired destination that God will be there. He is in charge of the show anyhow so aspire the journey! If you stop and think of all the times you wanted to give up but did not, what drove you to continue on your journey? It was through your faith in Him and the optimism you displayed that you were able to power through the unknown and unchartered territory, not knowing what the end would be.

Always remember that whatever you are feeling at a low time is temporary, and your feelings are a function of your thoughts. If you can change your thoughts, you can change your feelings, which helps you to feel better. Be kind to yourself through this process. The journey we call life is a process!

Reclaiming your purpose is both simple and complex. It may require a major career change, or it might also be solved through a renewed focus on how you spend your time at work. A sense of purpose tends to come from our values, rather than a specific skill or talent. A skill or talent, and the work we do is how we express our values or our purpose? Or both?

So, if you find yourself being burned out or wondering if education is still the career field for you, stop and ask yourself the following questions. What is my overall purpose in my work? What values am I expressing through what I do? What am I bringing to my work that enhances my life and the lives of students?

If you look at the definition of reclaim, it is to retrieve or recover something that was previously lost. Many educators tend to lose their passion for work after a few years. If we look closely, we can begin to realize it is much more personal. It is usually a deep uncertainty of not acting upon our best judgment. Moreover, meaning we do not do what we need to do to advance our careers and fuel our passion for the reason we entered into this challenging career field. We often get too comfortable and do what other people presume we should be doing, which allows us to become complacent in our everyday lives. I found my "why" again and it has reignited my passion for education. What is your "why?" Now is the time to reclaim your career!

"I've failed over and over and over again in my life
and that is why I succeed."
~Michael Jordan

Faith.Fear.Resilience Exercise

Resilience /rə'zilyəns/ resides within each and every one of us. We all have the capacity to overcome life-changing situations. Write down three difficult events you experienced that changed your life. Afterward, describe your personal strategy to overcome the situation. In the inspirational words of Jaeda Dewalt, "When we learn how to become resilient, we learn how to embrace the beautifully broad spectrum of the human experience."

1. Life-changing Situation:

_____

_____

_____

Personal Strategy:

_____

_____

_____

_____

_____

_____

_____

_____

2. Life-changing Situation:

_____

_____

_____

Personal Strategy:

_____

_____

_____

_____

_____

_____

_____

_____

_____

3. Life-changing Situation:

_____

_____

_____

Personal Strategy:

_____

_____

_____

_____

_____

_____

_____

_____

_____

WORKS CITED

Allegretto, S., Corcoran, S., and Mishel, L. (2004). *How Does Teacher Pay Compare? Methodological Challenges and Answers*. Washington, DC: Economic Policy Institute. Available at: https://www.epi.org/publication/books_teacher_pay/.

CommunicationWorks, L. (2011). *MetLife Survey of the American Teacher*. [online] Issuu. Available at: https://issuu.com/communicationworks/docs/metlife_teacher_survey_2010/34.

Crisis Prevention Institute. (2018). School Safety—It's Time to Give Teachers the Training They Deserve. Available at: https://www.crisisprevention.com/Blog/April-2018/Give-Teachers-the-Training-They-Deserve.

Daskal, L. (2019). *This is What Happens When Your Leadership Lacks Confidence - Lolly Daskal* | [online] Available at: https://www.lollydaskal.com/leadership/this-is-what-happens-when-your-leadership-lacks-confidence/ [Accessed 31 Dec. 2019].

Ferlazzo, L. (2018). *Response: "Building Relationships With Students Is the Most Important Thing a Teacher Can Do."* [online] Education Week - Classroom Q&A With Larry Ferlazzo. Available at: http://blogs.edweek.org/teachers/classroom_qa_with_larry_ferlazzo/2018/10/response_building_relationships_with_students_is_the_most_important_thing_a_teacher_can_do.html.

Gold, E. (n.d.). Recommended Citation. *The Journal of Sociology & Social Welfare. Jal Mehta. Reviewed by Eva Gold,* [online] 41(1), p.15. Available at: https://pdfs.semanticscholar.org/5abe/4eb83a8dfda3a0baff691c4c24f78eed24b1.pdf [Accessed 31 Dec. 2019].

National Institute of Education (2019). *Confident Teachers Make for Confident Learners | SingTeach | Education Research for Teachers.* [online] Available at: http://singteach.nie.edu.sg/issue56-research02/.

NEA Today. (2019). *Teacher Shortage Sends Retired Teachers Back to the Classroom.* [online] Available at: http://neatoday.org/2019/12/09/retired-teachers-returning-to-work/?_ga=2.266730636.305021372.1577819948-1985943654.1577819948 [Accessed 31 Dec. 2019].

Perry, C.M. (1999). Proactive Thoughts on Creating Safe Schools. *The School Community Journal* Vol. 9, No. 1, Spring/Summer 1999. Available at: http://www.adi.org/journal/ss01/Chapters/Chapter10-Perry.pdf.

Shanker Institute. (2015). *Developing Workplaces Where Teachers Stay, Improve, And Succeed.* [online] Available at: http://www.shankerinstitute.org/blog/developing-workplaces-where-teachers-stay-improve-and-succeed [Accessed 31 Dec. 2019].

U.S. Department of Education. (2017). Teacher Professional Development. Available at: https://nces.ed.gov/pubs2017/2017200.pdf.

www.ingramcontent.com/pod-product-compliance
Lightning Source LLC
Chambersburg PA
CBHW021348090426
42742CB00008B/782